# The Joyous Gift of
## Christmas

IMAGES of LIFE CELEBRATIONS

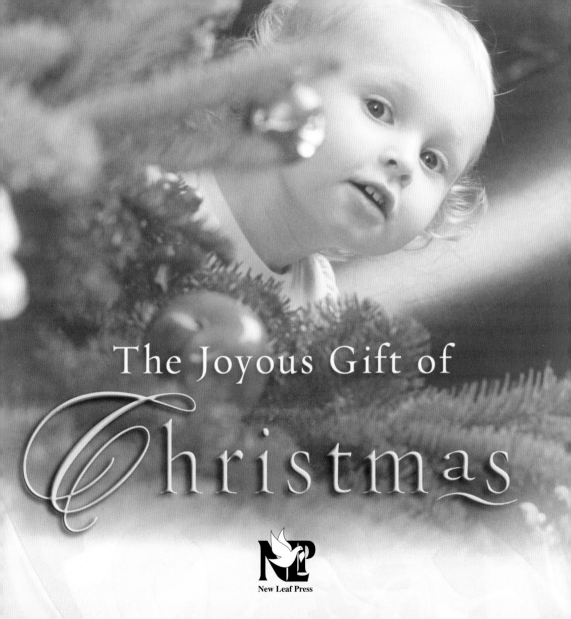

# The Joyous Gift of
# Christmas

New Leaf Press

**New Leaf Press**

# A special gift for you

To

_____

From

_____

# Introduction

A long time ago, in a distant land, a gift was given from a father to his children.

The gift was not placed under a tree, although a tree would be a part of the gift's destiny years later. The gift was not wrapped in bright, shiny paper, but in swaddling clothes. There were no twinkling lights, but there was a star that shone every night for weeks. There was no snow outside and no fireplace inside, but there was much loving warmth in the stable where the gift was given.

Although the gift cost the father no money, it was a priceless gift because it was the only one that the father had. The love and generosity of the father for his children became famous as the story spread throughout the world. It's the story of the joyous gift of Christmas. — Luke 2

*Train up a child in the way he should go: and when he is old, he will not depart from it.* — Prov. 22:6

A Christmas *candle* is a lovely thing;

It makes no noise at all,

But softly gives itself away;

While quite unselfish,

it grows small." – Eva K. Logue

*And the angel said unto them, Fear not: for behold, I bring you good tidings of great joy, which shall be to all people.* – Luke 2:10

*A gift is as a precious
stone in the eyes of
him that hath it.*

– Proverbs 17:8

The best of all gifts around any Christmas tree: the presence of a happy family all wrapped up in *each other*."

– Burton Hillis

Bless us Lord

# "Bless us Lord this Christmas,

With quietness of mind;

Teach us to be patient

And always to be kind."

– Helen Steiner Rice

*Rest in the Lord, and wait patiently for him.* – Psalm 37:7

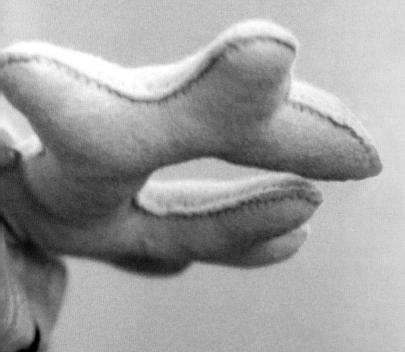

"*CHRISTMAS* is not a date. It is a *STATE OF MIND*."

– Mary Ellen Chase

# Gifts

"Christmas is based on an exchange of gifts:

the gift of God to man — **His Son**; and

the gift of man to God — when we first give

ourselves to God." —Vance Havner

*For God so loved the world, that he gave his only begotten Son, that whosoever believeth in him should not perish, but have everlasting life.* – John 3:16

"It is Christmas in the *heart*

that puts Christmas in the *air*." –W.T. Ellis

*Thou hast put gladness in my heart.* – Psalm 4:7

*And whoso shall receive one such little child in my name receiveth me. – Matthew 18:5*

*W*hatever else be lost among the years, let
us keep Christmas still a shining thing: Whatever
doubts assail us, or what fears, let us hold
close one day, remembering its poignant
meaning for the hearts of men.
Let us get back our childlike
faith again." – Grace Noll Crowell

*C*hristmas Eve . . .

For unto you is born this day in
the city of David a Saviour, which
is Christ the Lord. – Luke 2:11

. . . warmed your heart . . . filled it too, with a melody that would last *forever.*"

– Bess Streeter Aldrich

*Ye are the light of the world.*
— Matthew 5:14

God grant you the light in Christmas, which is faith; the warmth of Christmas, which is love; the radiance of Christmas, which is purity; the righteousness of Christmas, which is justice; the belief in Christmas, which is truth; the all of Christmas, which is Christ."

– Wilda English

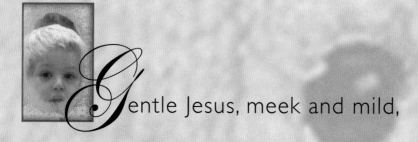

"Gentle Jesus, meek and mild,

Look upon a little child,

Pity my simplicity,

Suffer me to come to *thee*."

– Charles Wesley

*Suffer the little children to come unto me, and forbid
them not, for of such is the kingdom of God.* – Mark 10:14

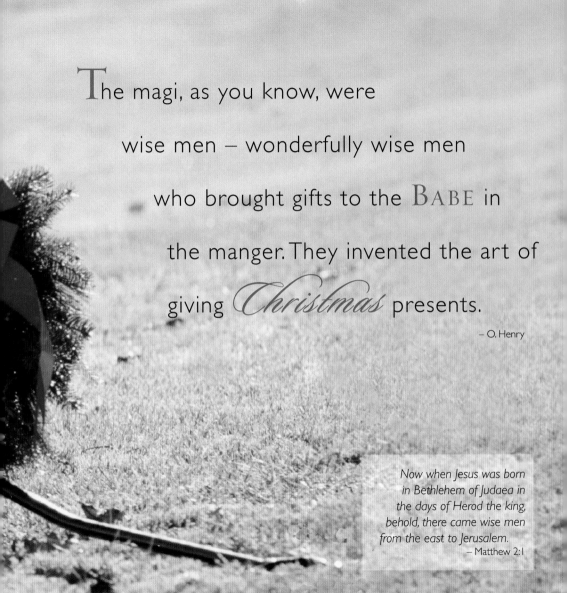

The magi, as you know, were wise men – wonderfully wise men who brought gifts to the BABE in the manger. They invented the art of giving *Christmas* presents.

– O. Henry

*Now when Jesus was born in Bethlehem of Judaea in the days of Herod the king, behold, there came wise men from the east to Jerusalem.*
– Matthew 2:1

"*Christmas* — that magic blanket that wraps itself about us, that something so intangible that it is like a fragrance. It may weave a spell of nostalgia. *Christmas* may be a day of feasting, or of prayer, but always it will be a day of remembrance — a day in which we think of everything we have ever loved."

— Augusta E. Rundel

Let thy fountain be blessed and rejoice
with the wife of thy youth. – Proverbs 5:18

Thanks be to God for His unspeakable Gift —
Indescribable
Inestimable
Incomparable
Inexpressible
Precious beyond words."

– Lois Lebar

*And suddenly there was with the angel a multitude of the heavenly host praising God, and saying, Glory to God in the Highest, and on earth peace, good will toward men.*
– Luke 2:13–14

S I N G S

Christmas gifts suggestions: to your enemy,
forgiveness; to your friend, your heart;
to a customer, service; to all, charity; to every child,
a good example; to yourself, respect. – Oren Arnold

*It is more blessed to give than to receive.* – Acts 20:35

*The* earth has grown

old with its burden of care,

But at **Christmas** it always is young." – Phillips Brooks

*Rejoice with them that do rejoice.*
– Romans 12:15

$\mathscr{P}$erhaps the best Yuletide

decoration is being wreathed in

*smiles.*"

– Unknown

*But joy cometh in the morning. – Psalm 30:5*

*I* stopped believing in Santa Claus when I was six. Mother took me to see him in a department store and he asked for **my** autograph."

– Shirley Temple

*G*od bless us every one!' said *Tiny Tim*,

the last of all.'' – Charles Dickens

*B*lessed is the **season** which engages the whole world in a conspiracy of love."

– Hamilton Wright Mabi

*Watch ye therefore, and pray always.* – Luke 21:36

*Christmas* waves a magic wand over this world, and behold, everything is softer and more *beautiful.* "

— Norman Vincent Peale

And into whatsoever house ye enter, first say, Peace be to this house. — Luke 10:5

"I know nobody likes me. Why do we have to have a holiday season to *EMPHASIZE* it?" – Charlie Brown

*A gift in secret pacifieth anger.*
– Proverbs 21:14

$\mathcal{N}$ever worry about the size of your

Christmas tree.

In the eyes of children, they are all

# 30 feet tall. "

—Larry Wilde

*For therein is the righteousness of God revealed from faith to faith: as it is written, The just shall live by faith.* – Romans 1:17

*S*leep, my child, and peace

attend thee,

All through the night;

Guardian angels God will lend thee,

All through the night;

Soft the drowsy hours are creeping,

Hill and dale in slumber steeping,

Love alone his watch is keeping —

All through the night." – Old Welsh Air

*And she brought forth her firstborn son, and wrapped him in swaddling clothes, and laid him in a manger; because there was no room for them in the inn.* – Luke 2:7

What do you call people

who are afraid of Santa Claus?

# Claustrophobic.

*If* there is no joyous way to give a festive gift, give love away." – Unknown

*Behold, we count them happy which endure.* – James 5:11

That were the sum of Christmas joys;
Mysterious secrets everywhere,
And snowflakes tumbling through the air.
And then, the greatest thrill of all,
On Christmas Eve, as great and small,
Behind the horses gay with bells,
Glide up the hills and down the dells
To Church!"

– Mary H. Beam

*For we have seen his star in the east, and are come to worship him.* – Matthew 2:2

$\mathcal{M}$ost of the time I like to think

That all my **childish** ways

Are but mementos of the past:

Forgotten yesterdays;

But once a year, at Christmastime

There comes a sudden change,

The years don't seem to count for much

— I'm just a child again."

– William A. Washburn

*And thou shalt have joy and gladness; and*
*many shall rejoice at his birth.* – Luke 1:14

"There has been only one *Christmas* — the rest are anniversaries." – W. J. Cameron

*And the child grew, and waxed strong in spirit, filled with wisdom: and the grace of God was upon him. – Luke 2:40*

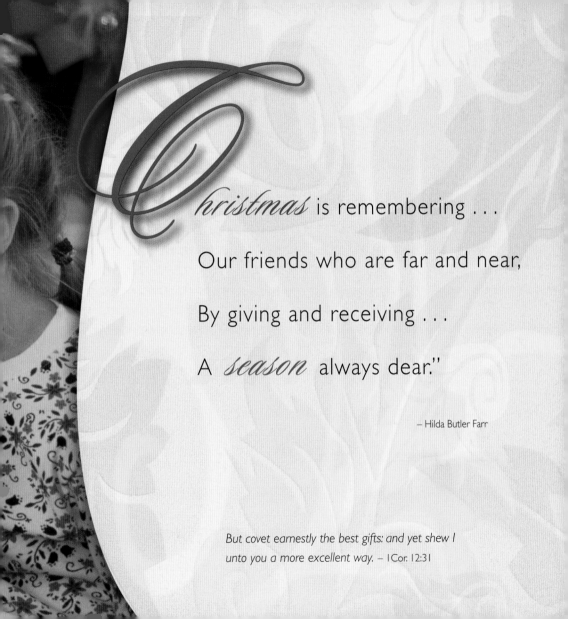

*Christmas* is remembering . . .

Our friends who are far and near,

By giving and receiving . . .

A *season* always dear."

– Hilda Butler Farr

*But covet earnestly the best gifts: and yet shew I
unto you a more excellent way.* – I Cor. 12:31

"Peace on earth will come to stay,

When we live Christmas every day."

— Helen Steiner Rice

*Peace on earth*

*That he would grant unto us, that we being delivered out of the hand of our enemies might serve him without fear.* – Luke 1:74

"*I* once bought my kids a set of batteries

for **Christmas** with a note on it saying,

'toys not included.' " – Bernard Manning

# Photo Credits

**Getty Images:**  1, 10, 12, 14, 18, 24, 50, 56, 59, 62, 64, 66, 69, 70

**SuperStock:**  22, 27, 28, 36, 40, 43, 46, 48, 53, 60

**ImageState:**  8, 25, 38, 54

**Corbis:**  16, 32, 68

**Veer:**  20, 44

**Christmas (Comstock):**  7, 9, 31, 34, 41

**Christmas Objects (Planet Art):**  11, 13